MINIATURES

and Other Poems

WESLEYAN POETRY

MINIATURES

and Other Poems

BARBARA GUEST

Wesleyan University Press

MIDDLETOWN, CONNECTICUT

Published by Wesleyan University Press, Middletown, CT 06459

© 2002 by Barbara Guest

Printed in the United States of America

5 4 3 2 1

CIP data appear at the back of the book

"I, too, am an ardent defender
of Miniature Pieces."

ANTON CHEKHOV

✻

Contents

MINIATURES

SHABBY BOOT

"There is a shabby boot

O whither does it wander?"

Earth has   gala momentum.

"Be not lachrymose,

tear-streaked.

You are out of reach

of fakirs.

On your boot

               the King of Naples inscribed

footprints of The Aeneid."

On the manuscript are Dido's tears,   from Dido.

BIRD OF ART

THERE CAME A CLOUD IT SETTLED ON YOUR
SHOULDER.
    The cloud seeks high culture, after Ovid.

        To soar through domes, bird of Art,
    Halfway to icy heaven.

        Halfway to heaven search in high space, in deep
    crevasse.

            Knighthood.

          Poesie be engendered after OVID.

SPIRIT TREE

LO! It shakes boughs Spirit Tree.

Plenty of wonder here and miraculum.

Pleaseth shade with lark!

Immortalis makes entry.
Small feet carry chalice, Domine.

Swete be sound and soothing.

Lady and gazelle, amitié.

TURRET

What is your version, raking hay, reading law
In turret, transferring documenta?

What is origin of miscellany, misdemeanor,

from whence doggerel?

Whose profile in margin

where small animals lie, toad, minnow, book of Saints,
olives.

NEGATIVE POSSIBILITY

It is not your physical appearance or hazelnut
hollowed out by sorrow,

or landslide of poetry.
Paying duty on one place,

language or tidal property.
Belonged to library of small estate,

Taxfree, built into house.

CAMISOLE

The heart knows.
climbs stair to reach
basket of Heaven.

wintry Heaven strikes arm.

Your viol shall release thee, is said.

Beyond steeple. Animals. Lather runs.
Fabric sewed into blood.

Moldy day. Leather gaiters. Warm camisole.
       Slow measure.

TINY FOREIGN TEARS

Tiny foreign tears in autumn,

Finnish architecture! Handshaking!

The right-handed cloud is
lower than the left
where a spirit hides.

In his dwelling Coleridge
handprints ghostly elaboration,

the notion of subject to enlarge,

he goes all year without.

Word akimbo,
lined with wool, even in far off place.

TRANSCRIPTION

Go sit, listen. Two feed earlobes, with wildermass. Slowly partake
of uncrippling. Part of transcription. Sleep of transcribing after long day
In honey cave, sans emotiveness.

There is lip descendant placed on wood for viol outside
witherglass. Here is plentiful lambswood fife for thine, we pass
upward in front of mere clumsy, Knight of Andorra and pony.

O sleep will be shiny apres plentiful unrehearsed   their sheaves, yon
Magnetic fleece nestling   while it chew
fertile green stone. Coxcomb be schon.

Alliance with bickering   be wrestled and
fielded on gold champs.

LOST SPEECH

Archaeology

        with a lift of brow and occupation,
some of it mixed, as in that speech germinated
on layers of limestone, protects a lost speech in thick
wood plundered.
        A search for past occupational diversions.

        Let history commandeer your tongue at this elevation.

        It is nothing to grow wings. To be La Favorita.

A girl wearing satin and wings makes a speech, then ventures
      outside, a cloak thrown over her shoulder. The Macedonians
know how to plunder, to thieve, yet they lifted La Favorita
      from the overturned ship, and send her back to the Lycians.

FIRST PRINTS

balanced on leaves green-toed
suspension
hard to pronounce,

to recall.   Pulled-up air evaporates.
here and in color.

Woman in field
light-toed.

Goddess category.

YESTERDAY

Light still glowing through the iced-over window, city
    silence and glow. Ice on Harbor Street.

    Twin points of light in darkened harbor.
Winter slumber. Lone tree. Shadow on empty beach.
Piece of ice. Daughter of an Elf.
               "Clouds afloat in Winter."

Red dots. Circular movement. Common life joined to emotion.
    Groaning roof sighed in sleep.

He wraps her hair around his wrist   a cloud   human hair
smothering the universe   in a mist dogs bark inside it.

Moon
in their sleep.

PILGRIMAGE

Start at beginning   in early morn
move through streams. Observe in district.

stripe of clown in vestibule,
brief rummage

Dove on mule cart.   Hand is homeless far from St. Jerome

and harping.   weightless, in Sacred Wood.

FINNISH OPERA

Grass grew long in the story.

Pieces clung to bedclothes. In the night he believed he grew taller.
Grass covered the dream of a serpent, eyes sunk in his head, tail of silk
clover. The dream translated into silver tone. More serpent heads and the
dream turned into an opera.

It was the opera that made the dreamer famous. Location of opera could be
in any country, could be Antarctica, more likely Finland, where they believe
in silk clover, it is gold in a land of starved desire for summer.

The opera had a clover leaf copied in porcelain by Aalto, the famous
designer, who sewed the clover leaf into a white curtain. He designed a
window for the man when he looks out to sea in his serpent costume.

This opera that begins with a dream traveled to Rome and Zagreb, traveled
across continents, once by camel. The travels became more famous than
the opera. People began to forget whether the grass really had grown long,
and where the serpent came from.

The opera was called by another name and included a gold limousine.
Somewhere in Oceania they added mermaid elves.

PHOTOGRAPHS

In the past we listened to photographs. They heard our voice speak.
Alive, active. What had been distance was memory.   Dusk came,
Pushed us forward,   emptying the laboratory   each night undisturbed by
Erasure.

In the city of X, they lived together. Always morose, her lips
soothed him. The piano was arranged in the old manner, light entered the
window, street lamps at the single tree.

Emotion evoked by a single light on a subject is not transferable to
photographs of the improved city. The camera, once
commented freely amid rivering and lost gutters of treeless parks or avenue.
The old camera refused to penetrate the unknown. Its heart was soft,
unreliable.

Now distributed is photography of new government building. We are
forbidden to observe despair silent in old photographs.

PETTICOAT

She ran down the middle of the road throwing her hands up to Heaven.
Longinus, Leviticus, mathematical wonder.
   She believed whole buildings might fall on top of her.

     Pollen filled the air.
It was her duty to plunder the ant of air, beasties of calico.
   The Morse Code arrived in petticoat blue, the steam engine.
   She read Liebnitz before she visted the pastor.

BLUE ARTHUR

Aroused from bed with movement around him.
Fasted and lay with malade.   Waited with poem
folded into sorrow.
Hollow, blue morning.

Cloth overhangs daytime

Kingdom of Blue Arthur.

Dismayed lightness.

Woman walks solitary arrayed in grey velveteen, doors open for her.

AUTOBIOGRAPHY

Underfoot is secure,
        part of made up plan.
        In middle ground,
   Coconut tree.

The coconut tree grows beside warm
        house, hard fruit has softened center.

In winter trees enter firm sand, barrels
        are protection from salt water.
most of the work elective.

        Air without salt is different, moves upward
from red evening sand.

        Bar of ivory light suspended,
           numbering of ivory bars.

NOISETONE

Each artist embarks on a personal search.
   An artist may take introspective refreshment from green.

Or so they say in Barcelona when air is dry.
   In our country it is a water sprinkler that hints, "rinsed green."
      Colors often break themselves into separate hues

   of noisetone.   In a Barcelona cabaret when green is overtaken,
it is stirred into the mint color of drink.

   The spirit is lifted among primary colors. Nine rows of color.
      The future writ in white spaces.

FOURTEENTH OF JULY

Automatically
        at lit dusk,

path of camera
veers into goats.

      Alpine

camera allowed, vendor of cockades,

        cockades, and nearby

  taper of
dried glass, mountain tapers.
Fire in snow, dazzle of film, raisin-charred, described later,
and under waterfall icicles.

       Walked with goat, shared
      scheme of Revolution,   thread   homespun
        In open place.

CHEKHOVIANA

En pointe in the *plié,* she greets monster sailing ship. Sky is overcast this day. Bell of last regime trembles in an overcoat. Worms wear old rings. "Here is where they were!" she says. "A bag of apricots hidden in the chair . . ." He listens to her sing "Bitter Avenue." Her boots are covered with caravan dust, broken seams.

Roofs fall in, no grapes grow in the harbor.

They only have their skin and old satin shoes. "It's the luck of the road," she moans, and puts her hand on his cheek. "Look at our russet wind."

COAL

The black curtain has fallen over the moon, yet stars are out tonight. Dust falls through the curtain. We are asleep. Night descends into another part of the house, coal shifts in the bin.

My grandfather shuffled the coal veins that come from the deep shoulder. My eyes are closed, flecks of coal fall onto my cheek. He brushes them away. He brushes my shoes with a little shoe brush. Soon his eyes are closed. His eyes shine red in his kingdom. I view the coal God through dust, darkest dust.

COLONIAL HOURS

Slow moving and daybreak,

an eyelash trembles. Cat in mouse coat and thunder, the lane shivers. A
branch falls as she listens. Weary of effervescence, pickling langours and
knitted on the way to Princeton in a phaeton, dark blue splashed, mud from
early rains. Bon jour to the Count. 'bonjour' Benjamin Franklin, we've
memorized the court order, legalized the tunes. An
odd evening. Dark in the middle where the berries stood.
The spinet was out of tune.

SOUND AND STRUCTURE

"Sound leads to structure." Schönberg.

On this dry prepared path walk heavy feet.
This is not "dinner music." This is a power structure,
heavy as eyelids.
Beams are laid. The master cuts music for the future.

Sound lays the structure. Sound leaks into the future.

MUSICIANSHIP

How far are you going in the culture program? Lizt draws nearer. Wagner overwhelmed us in that last demonic song.

Where the snowline fell on its supple track, people lost their maps in advanced culture. And the faces, on the back row singing: rare tonalism, lying on its sides like a walrus, chords broken and chewed in liberation.

PATHOS

Arms flutter close to the body, skating on pure ice, harmonious composition, —

body in mellifluous line —

face in profile witheld itself, thin smile,
self approval.

Lithe her romp!

lithesome her romp upon the indignation of ice.

She is falling!

Shiver of the fallen,
of the tulle skirt.

Disarrangement of composition,

Snow falling from tree.

So young in this electric world —,

something Katya needs to know. Something is needed,

fiction is overturned.

Something she must know about hazard, what spills out —

— *disturbance,* — *pathos.*

Equilibrium never fixed —

losing momentum in the trials — boot tossed away,
a gesture she made.

Making difficulties for herself   in the wrong direction.
Fear of the word, haunting of fear —

      the word passed through that haunting.

      Weight of the useless word,
          mirror moving backward,

   impromptu surface of the alphabet when she fell sideways

with irascible measure — the pit of the plum
rolled onto ice,   and her silhouette   merged quickly
        with ice in that chapter.

Opened the entrance door,

and make-believe arrived   with a doll on its surface,

arrived with the soil of the moon,   it was impermanent

living with shifted screen life.

Lived not for pleasure,   to hear the cry

in a small coil
of ice.

And heard through the oak panel —,

amazing to listen to speech
by way of adulthood.

To articulate velvet,

without noise or spectacle.

Life in that eccentric balloon.

To scribble ice figures,

and drink out of the cup when bolder.
The electric world sends its current through her legs,
a global concern for her being.

The globe is drawn into this, and the frills,
the sorrow of falling

into an historical position, the legs will finish
this position, music
uses up the irresistible current, lived
with the shifting screen.

Lived not for pleasure,   to hear the harp-like
cry in a coil,

to live in an eccentric balloon.

To scribble across ice

and drink from an orange cup.   When they were nearer

historical legs used up this position,

falling down historical legs, anxious writing.

Foreignness enters the hallway in the Berlioz —

hinting at the fable
                    resisting her.

Do they wonder at her pathos/ dressed in tulle,
    athletically inclined on jumping bars.

                            One at a time

        misleading her./

She is part of *the moment*/ unrequited amour/

                            icing machine.

    This motion in her eyes,

going outside,   the red brook
            flowed into her eyes, winsome eyes,

            drawstring of light.

BLURRED EDGE

It appears

a drama of   exacting dimension.

Anguished figure,

reign of terror.

Craft and above all

the object within.

Softness precedes

blurred edge.

A hint disappears   inside the earlier one.

Softness still nudging,

A different temperament,

inside an earlier plan.

Upon this stool is draped material
arabesque of an iron stool,

bare bones of the iron seat.

The arrangement of objects   announced

    more firmly than before.

       Observation.   Candor,

    where candor approaches the cube.

Dark siphon bottle   mood

           of blurred edge.

Life permitted no privilege

no exegesis
no barnyard door.   The feathered visage   the domed hat

allowed no strange air or music.

An attempt to get beyond the arrangement,

the vibration of a peculiar touch.

It changes between eye and alarm,

the hibiscus,

more gifted.

Part of the tension,

is illusory.

A hint of what was going to be.

Covering and uncovering necessary.

Self pouring out of cloudedness.

If views of the lower body

do not conform,
        a risk of being exposed,

        Rain and altitude.

This is not sand, it is drama.

The anguished figure, sand blew away
that armor. A look   extends the blur.

        Other   creatures alive,
word exchanged for meaning,
        moment of descriptiveness.

        Sand blows away

        the carapace,
                in the distance,
    figure passing,
        unworded distance at edge.

ABOUT THE AUTHOR

Barbara Guest has published twenty-one volumes of poetry since 1960, as well as a novel entitled *Seeking Air* (1996) and the biography *Herself Defined: The Poet H.D. and Her World* (1984). She has earned many awards, including the 1999 Robert Frost Medal for Distinguished Lifetime Achievement from the Poetry Society of America.

LIBRARY OF CONGRESS CATALOGING-IN-PUBLICATION DATA

Guest, Barbara.

Miniatures and other poems / Barbara Guest.

   p.   cm. — (Wesleyan poetry)

ISBN 0–8195–6595–4 (cloth : alk. paper) — ISBN 0–8195–6596–2 (pbk. : alk. paper)

I. Title. II. Series.

PS3513.U44 M46 2002

811'.54—dc21   2002006946